A PLUI

HERE'S A BRILLIANT IDEA

The Brothers McLeod are an award-winning creative team who have worked with Disney, DreamWorks, and the BBC.

PLUME
An imprint of Penguin Random House LLC
375 Hudson Street
New York, New York 10014

First published in Great Britain in 2015 by LOM Art,
an imprint of Michael O'Mara Books Limited

Library of Congress Cataloging-in-Publication Data

Names: Brothers McLeod, creator.
Title: Here's a brilliant idea : 104 activities to unleash your creativity /
The Brothers McLeod.
Other titles: Here is a brilliant idea
Description: New York, New York: Plume, an imprint of Penguin
Random House LLC, [2016]
Identifiers: LCCN 2016023196 | ISBN 9780735215382 (paperback)
Subjects: LCSH: Creation (Literary, artistic, etc.)—Humor. | Creative
thinking—Humor. | BISAC: SELF-HELP / Creativity. | LANGUAGE
ARTS & DISCIPLINES / Composition & Creative Writing. | HUMOR /
Form / Comic Strips & Cartoons.
Classification: LCC BF411 .B76 2016 | DDC 153.3/50207—dc23
LC record available at https://lccn.loc.gov/2016023196

Printed in the United States of America
1   3   5   7   9   10   8   6   4   2

Designed by Design 23

HERE'S A BRILLIANT IDEA

104 Activities to Unleash Your Creativity

The Brothers McLeod

A PLUME BOOK

Introduction

Hi, I'm Greg.

I'm Myles.

He's a writer.

And he's a drawy man.

An illustrator!

Whatever.

This is our book to help you come up with ideas.

Basically, our goal is to help you fill this book with words and pictures that might inspire you to go away and create something wonderful.

If one day you look down at this book, creased, well-worn, filled with doodles and scratchy notes, and say, "What a load of nonsense!," then we have done our job!

 The book includes some insights into how we come up with ideas.

But also there are lots of silly exercises to help kick-start your creative mind and silence your inner critic.

You can work your way through the book, or just dip in at random when you feel in need of inspiration.

Some of the exercises involve drawing, some writing, others are just meant to spark ideas and set you off.

Let us begin with . . .

A BRIEF HISTORY OF IDEAS

* Part One *

I am always
doing that which
I cannot do, in
order that I may
learn how to do it.
—**Pablo Picasso**

Write down here all the things you really want to do, but haven't mastered yet. Draw a picture for each one.

— I'd love to master
speaking Russian!

Привет, брат! —

UNDISCOVERED DINOSAUR

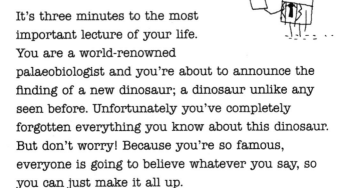

It's three minutes to the most important lecture of your life. You are a world-renowned palaeobiologist and you're about to announce the finding of a new dinosaur; a dinosaur unlike any seen before. Unfortunately you've completely forgotten everything you know about this dinosaur. But don't worry! Because you're so famous, everyone is going to believe whatever you say, so you can just make it all up.

Please, Professor, tell us about your new discovery here:

Dinosaur's
scientific name: . . . .

Height: . . . .

Weight: . . . .

Length: . . . .

Diet: . . . .

Habitat: . . . .

Other remarkable features: . . . .

. . . .

. . . .

Now draw the dinosaur:

Fill in the speech bubbles:

Design your own carpet:

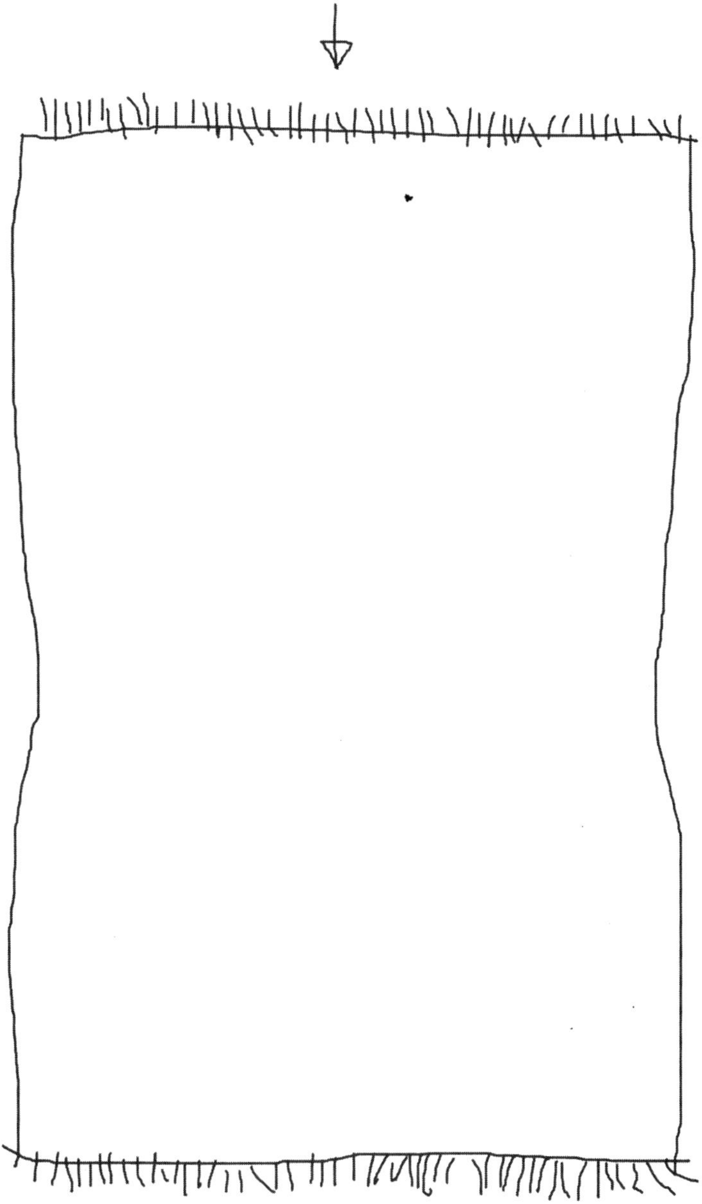

Squiggle picture—find some characters:

Now try your own.
Tip: draw the lines quickly and freely.

Give the characters heads:

Give these characters bodies:

FIRST LINES FOR YOUR
GREAT NOVEL

She left the cut flowers in the fish tank; it was her way of saying . . .

May 10, 1942. I have just returned from a meeting with the Bulldogs and the Dachshunds. I feel . . .

At last we have unlocked the formula, so now we can . . .

The throne was shaped like an egg and was painted . . .

Montague was a tall, willowy gentleman who would have cut a most handsome figure were it not for the gigantic twin boils beneath his pouting lips. He had the air of someone who . . .

Continue one of the stories:

_____

_____

_____

_____

_____

_____

_____

_____

_____

_____

_____

_____

_____

_____

Add your own pictures to the panels:

PREDICT THE FUTURE
EXERCISE FADS

Hyena Chess
Sewer Swimming
Chimney Hop
Grizzly Bear Yoga

Now it's your turn:

1. _____
2. _____
3. _____
4. _____
5. _____

Make up satisfyingly insulting nicknames for ex-girlfriends:

Mirror Worm   Sweaty Yeti

    Roboknickers

Realized Mythical Evil of Worldwide Doom

        Firetongue the Ever Right

    Princess Pondlife

        Whingermonger

_____

_____

_____

_____

_____

_____

_____

_____

Make up satisfyingly insulting nicknames for ex-boyfriends:

Vest Mule   Sockish

    Two Pants   Waxy Dribbler

       Tentacle Tom

     Neil Anderthal

    Octopus Touch

               Face Blooper

_____

_____

_____

_____

_____

_____

_____

_____

Where do ideas come from?
Part One.

What exactly are
ideas, Greg?

Well, Myles, some
people believe they
are tiny fairy burps
that invade our
thoughts.

But others say they
are invisible worms
that sing directly into
our brain cells.

I see.

Some theorists
suggest ideas are the
faint whisperings of
aliens communicating
on a quantum level.

I hadn't heard that.

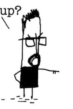

Still more people
say that ideas aren't
real and that nothing
really exists.

Are you just
making this up?

That seems
particularly
unhelpful.

There are some that say ideas are bursts of inspiration creating images in your mind, influenced by your experiences and your hopes and dreams.

That seems the most likely, if somewhat obvious?

Look, they were just ideas about where ideas come from.

Ideas about ideas?

Yes. I wonder where those ideas about ideas came from?

Ugh. My mind aches.

RANDOM HAIKU POEMS

(5 SYLLABLES, 7 SYLLABLES, THEN 5)

Try creating poems with two friends.

Write a line each. Cover it as you go so you can't see what each other has written for your line. Here are a few we made earlier:

The door is open.
Pilots painted the room green,
I called him "student."

David calls him George.
They make him cry and whistle,
I get the watch fixed.

I elected her.
That announcer keeps things clean.
Guards kept the room warm.

____ ____ ____ ____ ____

____ ____ ____ ____ ____ ____ ____

____ ____ ____ ____ ____

____ ____ ____ ____ ____

____ ____ ____ ____ ____ ____ ____

____ ____ ____ ____ ____

____ ____ ____ ____ ____

____ ____ ____ ____ ____ ____ ____

____ ____ ____ ____ ____

Things You Might Like to Try If They Weren't a Crime

Smashing up a Ferrari with a
sledgehammer

Boxing with kangaroos

Naked public trampolining

Tasering people with audible music
coming from their headphones

Using the Ejector Seat function
for noisy people
in the quiet car of the train

Eating a swan
Eating a turtle
Eating a swan stuffed with a turtle

What would you do?

_____

_____

_____

_____

_____

_____

_____

_____

_____

_____

_____

_____

Coloring in

Color in the shapes below using complementary colors:

Shapes

Create your own dog breeds using the shapes below:

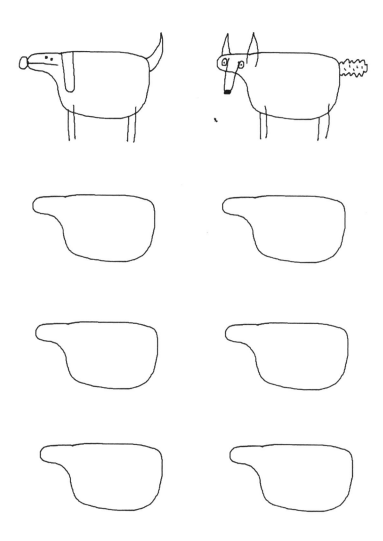

Bowl of words

Write a list of random words on a specific subject and
then pick out three at a time from a bowl
to generate ideas.

Write your three words below. When you put these
random words together, what do you think about?

CITYSCAPE

A line . . .

Some shapes . . .

Add detail . . .

Try one for yourself below.

Perspective

By simply drawing a few lines you can create a twisted perspective image.

Try it below:

Poetry of the pocket

Greg A while back, Myles went to a poetry workshop.

Myles It was given in the classroom where Shakespeare went to school.

Greg Cool!

Myles One of the tasks was to write a poem about something from our pocket.

Greg What was in your pocket?

Myles A lens cloth.

Greg A fascinating topic.

Myles Actually it was surprising how much I could write about it. I'd had it for ages and it made me think about what it meant to me to wear glasses.

So . . . what is in your pocket? Write a poem about it below.

Coloring in

Sometimes it's good just to color in a repetitive image; it's very therapeutic. You can color the strange creatures in the same or differently.

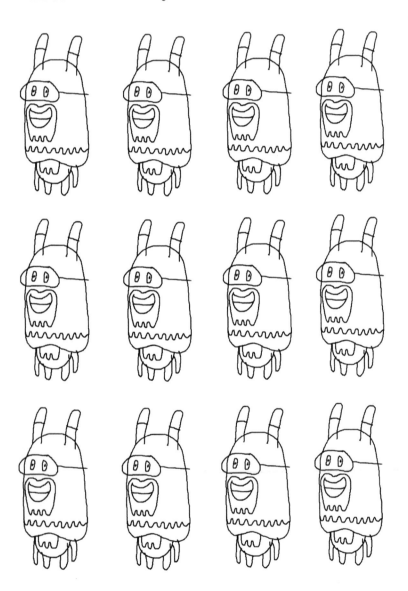

Character blanks

Using one shape you can create multiple characters.
What can you come up with?

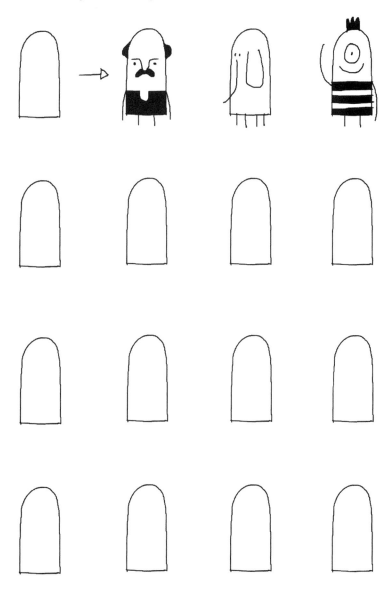

Doodle swirls

**Draw a swirl—do it
quick, then doodle.**

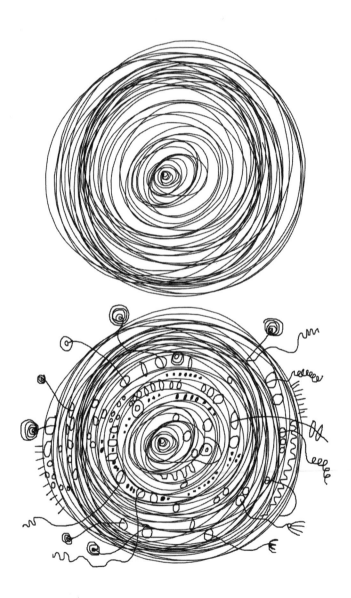

Do your version below:

HOW NOT TO HAVE IDEAS

Stay in bed.

Just five more minutes.

Ideas come from many different places.

Some ideas come from within. How you feel at any given moment will affect the ideas you have.

Draw an image below that matches how you feel right now:

DESIGN yOUR vERY OWN tOtEM POLE

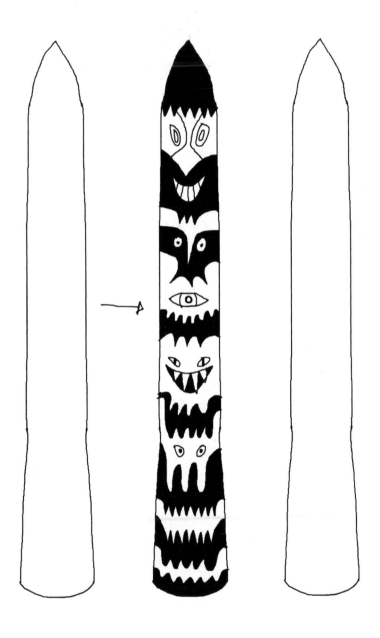

IT'S OKAY TO DAYDREAM.

COLOR ME IN

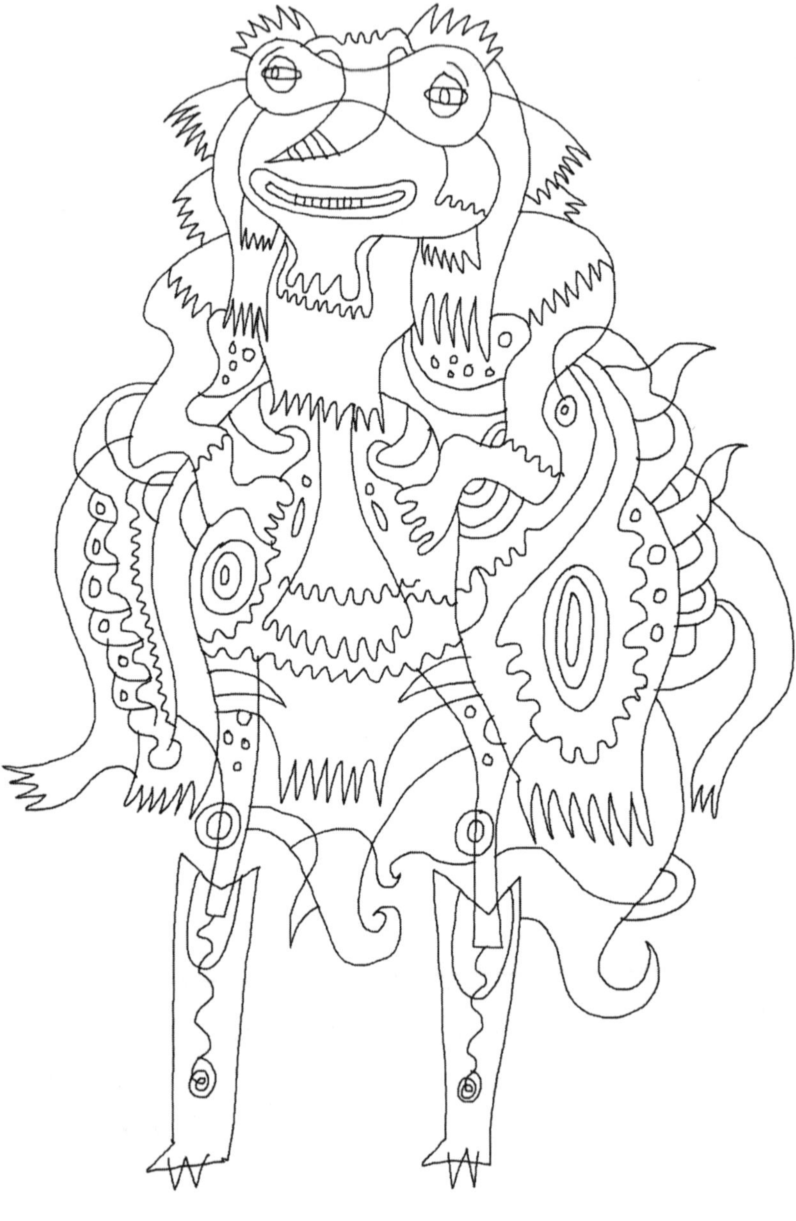

Create a forest:

Draw circles and ovals, then draw in tree trunks and some grass. Add some color.

CHARACTER BACKSTORIES ARE SO BORING

Greg   Myles, let's create a character!

Myles   Boring.

Greg   Oh yeah. Boring!

Myles   Boring! Boring!

BOORRRING!
BORRRRING!

Sometimes coming up with characters can be really dull. There's some handy checklists you can find on the Web that help you to flesh out a character.

Like, what's their name?

What's their politics?

What matters to them?

What's their inside leg measurement?

Do they recycle?

These are very, very useful.

And totally boring to fill in.

So instead, here's a really short and daft checklist to help to create a character.

This is based on something Myles did when he studied screenwriting, but with a couple of twists in it!

First name: _____

Last name: _____

Where do they live? _____

What is their favorite cheese? _____

Where do they go on vacation? _____

If they were a color, what would they be?

_____

If they were an animal, what would they be?

_____

They have a secret. What is it?

_____

_____

_____

_____

_____

There's no pressure to come up with something amazing. Just write down whatever comes into your head, however silly.

We did this at a kids' festival once. They created the cutest, pinkest fairy character, but when we asked, "She has a secret, what is it?," one child piped up with the best answer you can imagine: "She secretly hates herself." Now that's drama.

OPPOSITES

Okay. Look at the character you created on the previous page. Now write a character who is the complete opposite.

First name: _____

Last name: _____

Where do they live? _____

What is their favorite cheese? _____

Where do they go on vacation? _____

If they were a color, what would they be?

_____

If they were an animal, what would they be?

_____

They have a secret. What is it?

_____

_____

_____

_____

Now write a conversation between your two characters where they argue over the best way to eat a doughnut.

THE BEST WAY TO EAT A DOUGHNUT:

_____

_____

_____

_____

_____

_____

_____

_____

_____

_____

_____

_____

_____

_____

CONSEQUENCES

Greg   Myles, do you remember when we were kids, we played that game "Consequences"?

Myles   Oh yeah! With Grandma. With a piece of paper that you folded over?

Greg   Yeah! So you wrote the man's name, then folded it over, then wrote the lady's name, then wrote where they met, what he said to her, what she said to him, and then what happened.

Myles   And each time you passed it to the next person so you didn't know how the story would play out until you unfolded it all at the end?

Greg   That is actually the most fun you can have with a scrap of paper and a pen.

Myles   It is!

Greg   We should do that . . .

His name: _____

Her name: _____

Where they met: _____

What he said to her: _____

What she said to him: _____

What happened next: _____

_____

_____

_____

_____

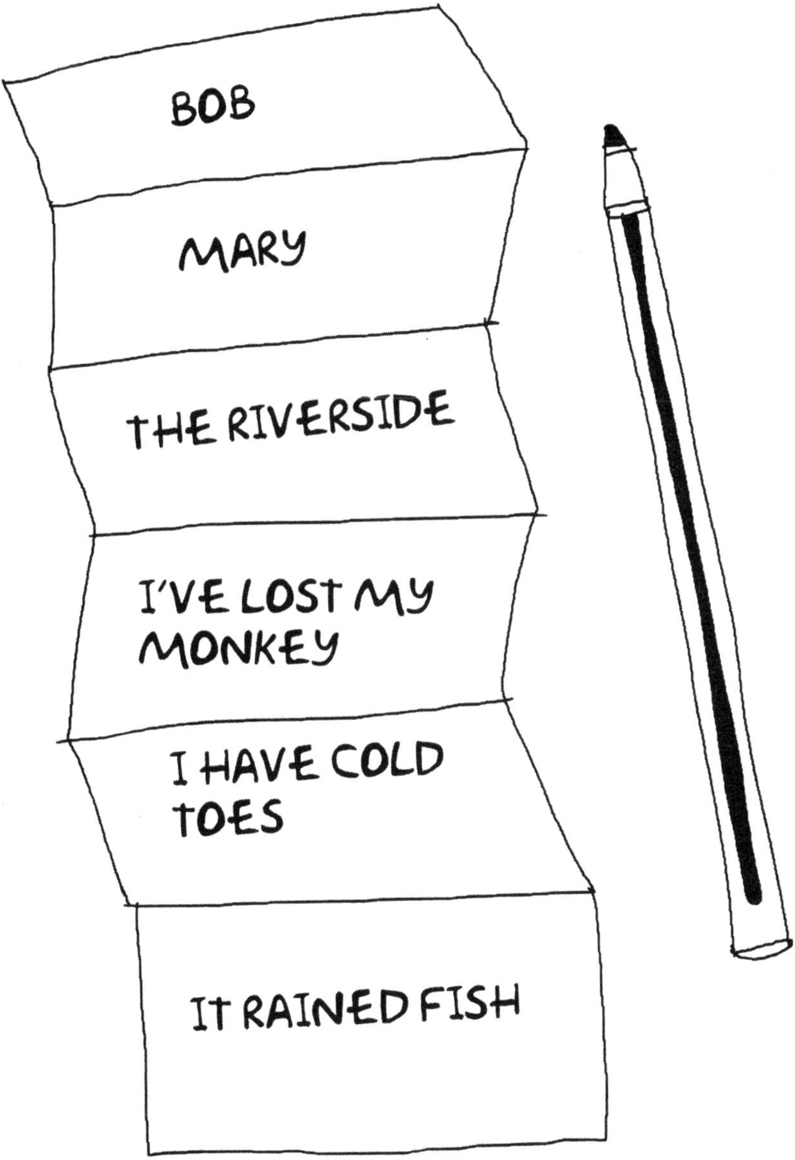
BOB
MARY
THE RIVERSIDE
I'VE LOST MY MONKEY
I HAVE COLD TOES
IT RAINED FISH

Play "Consequences" with a friend, then fill in your answers below:

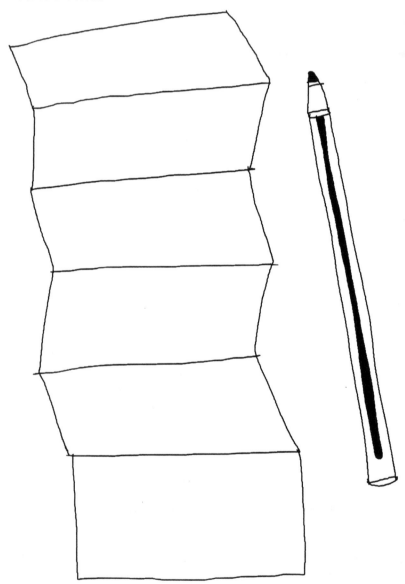

HOW NOT TO HAVE IDEAS

Watch the television.

I'll create something
amazing right after
this.

FOUR CORNERS

When we started out we made an animation for a "change management" company. It was used to demonstrate the different personalities you find in a workplace and how they can work against one another. They identified four types of managers: autocrats, democrats, risk-takers, and people who were strictly by-the-book. The amazing thing for us at the time was that sticking those four characters together in any situation created conflict and therefore drama.

Draw them and try to bring out their character in their expression and how they dress.

Autocratic **Democratic**

Risk-taker **By-the-book**

FOUR CORNERS

Write a scene with the four character types from the previous page trying to take charge of a situation using their preferred way of looking at the world. What's the situation? Hmm! They've lost a pencil. Or they need to defuse a galaxy-destroying bomb. Take your pick.

_____

_____

_____

_____

_____

_____

_____

_____

_____

_____

_____

_____

Sometimes I just
think I'm re-creating
stuff I've already
seen.

Yeah, finding your
own style can be
tricky. That's why
it's important
to listen to your
inner voice.

Sounds a bit
creepy.

It can be difficult to find it. But you'll
know it when you do because you will
feel a real connection with whatever
it is you are creating. It will feel
honest and truthful and you may even
feel a sense of release . . . like you've
understood something important
about yourself.

So you're saying I
should listen to the
voices in my head?

LISTEN TO THE VOICES IN YOUR HEAD!

COLLABORATION

Greg   For this section you'll need to find someone else.

Myles   A fellow creative!

Greg   Maybe someone who has different skills from you.

Myles   For example, Greg likes to draw and play drums.

Greg   Whereas Myles likes to dress up as a wizard.

Myles   Er. No. Actually I write words for a living, and I can play guitar. A bit.

Greg   And you dress up as a wizard.

Myles   Technically, that's just a robe.

Greg   Wizard.

Myles   Fine. But wizards can get pretty creative, you know.

Draw a character here:

Now ask your fellow creative to create a character profile for your character. What's their name? Where do they live? What's their job? If they were a color, what would it be? Or an animal? Do they have secrets? What are they?

_____

_____

_____

COLLABORATION

Okay, this time let's do the same thing as the previous page, but the other way around.

Write down a character profile here.

_____

_____

_____

_____

_____

_____

_____

_____

_____

_____

_____

_____

_____

Now ask your fellow creative to draw a
picture inspired by your words.

Greg   There's no right or wrong way to start creating characters.

Myles   Sometimes we get inspired by a picture in Greg's sketchbook.

Greg   Other times we'll start with a bunch of ideas for characters and then have to work out how they look afterward.

Myles   The main thing is to play around.

Greg   Our ninja character Fuggy started life as a sketch.

Myles   What is it with you and ninjas?

Greg   Nothing.

Myles   Hang on. You think it's weird I like dressing up. But I've seen you dress like a ninja!

Greg   I don't like dressing up.

Myles   But you do dress up as a ninja, don't you?

Greg   It's not really dressing up. It's just black clothes with a balaclava.

Myles   I knew it.

Given a choice, who would you dress up as?
Draw yourself below:

Draw to the music

Use a pen or pencil to accent and describe a piece of music. Don't worry about it being a picture of anything; just let yourself go and scribble. Keep going until the page is full.

Find a piece of **classical music** and draw your
picture below:

FANTASY FRIENDS

*Here are some of
our fantasy friends:*

Serge

Agent 88

Cyclops

Nigel

Ian

Faun

Spear

Spike

Who are your fantasy friends?

SELF-DOUBT

PART ONE

Everyone experiences self-doubt about their creative work.

Even if you've been doing it your whole life. It's normal.

Also, some of what you come up with will be rubbish. That is normal. It's allowed.

If you do not experience any self-doubt and think everything you do is from the mind of an unrelenting genius . . . then you are an egotistical moron.

George Lucas managed to create *Star Wars*, one of the most popular story worlds ever.

But he also created *Howard the Duck*.

You know, I never actually watched that.

No one did.

SELF-DOUBT

PART TWO

Believe in yourself.

Not in a religious way, that would be odd.

If you keep creating stuff, you will get better at it.

You will also begin to understand what gives you the most joy.

Don't worry too much whether anyone else likes it.

You have to like it first.

If you like it, others will like it too.

You'll find your audience.

There's no point creating stuff you don't like.

You'll end up with an audience of people with whom you have no connection.

This happened to a famous comedian. He was doing a particular style of comedy. Then he overheard his audience members talking while he was in a stall in the bathroom. He realized he didn't even like these people. Why was he trying to make them laugh? He decided to reinvent his comedy and find his people.

I've run out of ideas.
No, you haven't.
No, I really have.
No, you really haven't.

Fill in the speech bubbles:

SPEND A DAY WITHOUT ELECTRICITY.

HOW NOT TO HAVE IDEAS

Check out your phone, then your computer, then your tablet, then go back to checking out your phone. And so on.

SPLAT!

Use the ink splats below to create some characters or objects:

What's in the hole?

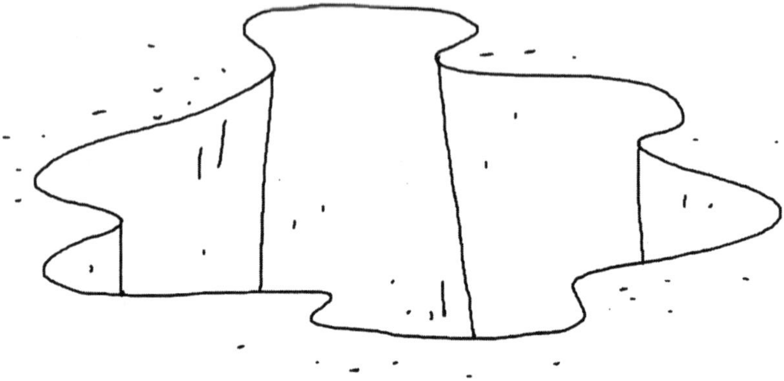

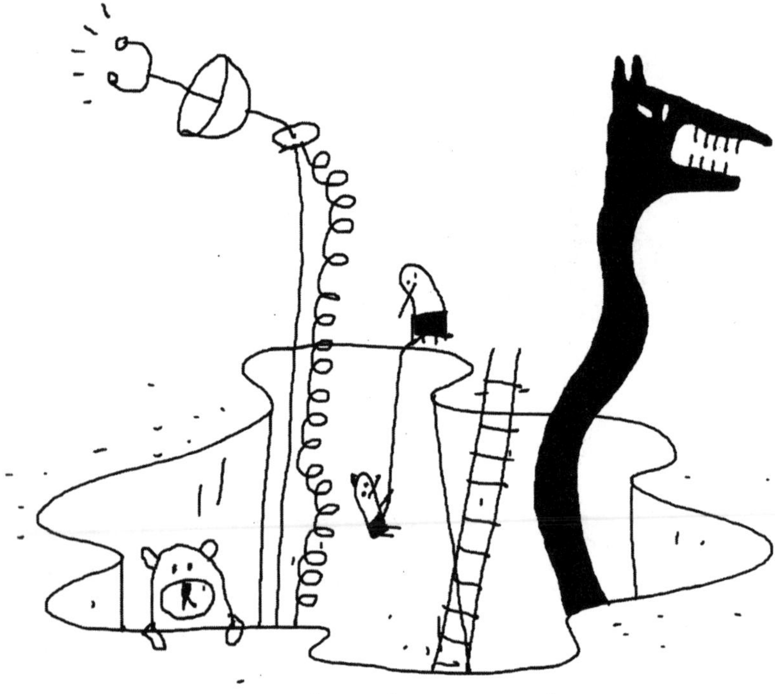

What's in your hole?

Complete the story

Derick picked up the watermelon and threw it off the cliff. He watched it fall and land in . . .

_____

_____

_____

_____

_____

_____

_____

_____

_____

_____

_____

_____

_____

_____

HOW TO HAVE IDEAS

Try silence. It's underrated. If you are surrounded by silence your brain might just decide to fill the void with ideas.

GO TO THE
NEAREST TOWN TO
YOU THAT YOU'VE
NEVER BEEN TO.

Tell a story in six speech bubbles:

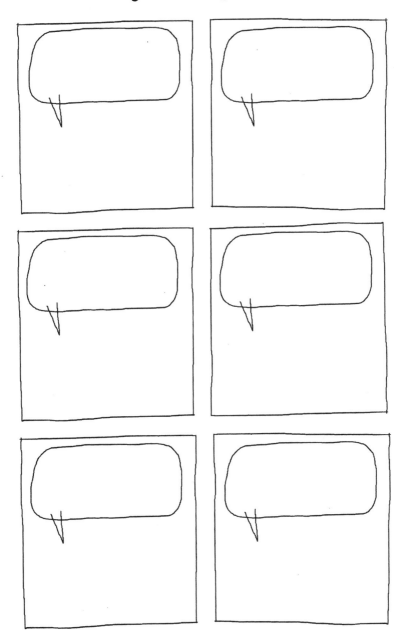

Where do ideas come from?

We did a little project for the Royal Shakespeare Company a while back featuring some poems and pictures about this exact question. We identified these seven sources of inspiration. See what ideas they inspire in you.

BIRTHPLACE

DREAMS

THEFT

LOVE

ANGER

DEATH

FROLICS

Birthplace

Where were you born? You probably think it's the most unremarkable of all places. But to someone half the world away it would seem alien, interesting, different. There are things about the place you grew up in that influence you. Shakespeare knew all about the plants and birds around his native Stratford-upon-Avon. They featured in his plays years later. Write about the place you were born in or grew up in. Try and see what makes it remarkable. How has it influenced you?

_____

_____

_____

_____

_____

_____

_____

_____

_____

_____

Dreams

Dreams are great because you can be
walking down a road, then sitting, you can
be yourself, then suddenly the opposite sex,
and then a child again. Anything is possible. Of course,
often our dreams slip away very quickly. So the way to
capture dreams is to have a pad and pen ready by your
bedside. When you wake up, immediately grab them and
write down the images in your head. Perhaps they will
inspire you. Perhaps there's something on your mind that
you can work into your artistic life. Or perhaps you'll just
realize how weird your mind is.

Of course there's another meaning to dreams—your
personal dreams, your ambitions, your bucket list. What
are these things? What are they?

Why aren't you writing about these things?

You care about them!

Do it!

Frolics

Trying to be creative can become a task, a drudge, especially if you put yourself under too much pressure. Well, stop it!

We come up with some of our best ideas when we allow ourselves to have fun.
To be carefree.
To be silly.
To say anything we feel like saying.

Being creative should be fun. You're allowed to enjoy yourself.

Don't put yourself under heaps of pressure to be the next William Shakespeare or the next Michelangelo.

This kind of thinking is especially fun with a creative partner or team.

You can encourage each other.

Make each other laugh.

Afterward you can worry about whether you created anything that you'd like to take further.

Theft

Plagiarism is theft.

Yeah, if you just scrubbed out our name on the front cover of this book and wrote yours there, that would be bad. So don't do it, all right?

But there is a different kind of theft that is perfectly acceptable. Think of how many King Arthur stories there've been! All those writers stealing the original story and reinventing it. William Shakespeare took a bunch of old plays and worked his magic on them. He made them his own. He made them better.

So is there an old story that you love? (Remember to check that it's out of copyright.) All the old fairy stories are there for you to reinvent! For example, *Cinderella* . . . she's a pretty passive character in the old story. She obediently does all the chores for her stepmother, then out of the blue a fairy godmother turns up and sorts out her life. Can you think of a way to reinvent that story?

Maybe she has a bazooka in your version? Maybe the fairy godmother is the stepmother in disguise?

What? How does that work? It'd be like a conspiracy thriller but with more pumpkins. I like it.

This ties into a creative crisis problem some folks have. Do you worry you're telling the same story as someone else? Drawing the same stuff as others? Well, stop it. You are you and you will tell it your way.

Tell the story of Cinderella here—
but do it your way:

Love

Who do you love?
What attracts you to them?
When did you fall in love?
Where?

If you were going to create something for them, just them, an audience of one, what would it be?

Sometimes it can really help to work out what a story or picture or poem or film should be if you just focus on making it for one person you know really well.

What is your brilliant idea for creating something for a special person?

ANGER

What makes your blood boil?

Take action now.

Write a story about it.

Draw a picture.

Fill it full of opinion and spirit.

Now pretend you felt exactly the opposite.

Pretend you held the opposite views.

Why would you? What would be the best arguments for thinking that way?

This is a good way to start thinking about antagonists in stories!

The best antagonists are the ones who almost convince you they are right.

DEATH

Whoa! Big topic.

Yes. When you think about it, all creativity is about death.

Which is the opposite of death, so it's still about death.

Or about life.

You're bleak.

No. Just deep and meaningful.

Mmm.

Anyway. Death features a lot in creativity. From a fictional point of view it adds peril and high stakes to drama. From a personal point of view it forces us to think about what really matters to us. There are lots of ways we can think about death for creative purposes.

Which deceased figure from history most inspires you?

If you were going to die in a year and you had time for one last big creative project, what would you do?

Is there someone you loved who has died? If you were to create something in their memory, what would that be?

Fill the plant pots with plants:

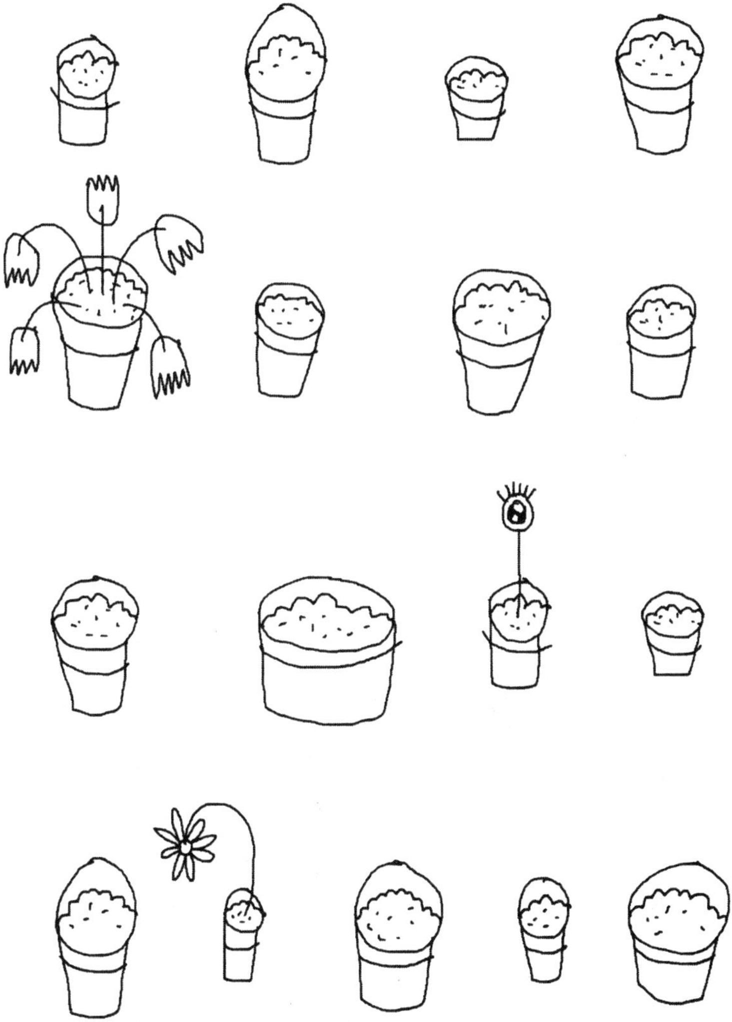

Creative space

Instead of trying to create stuff in your home,
studio, or office, find another place that's good
for creativity. We like to go to a hotel library bar
around the corner from our office. We'll often have
breakfast and coffee there. There are no computers.
It's quiet. It's a great place to chat through ideas
and come up with new ones.

What would be your ideal quiet place to think?
Write about it or draw it below:

This creature needs some features:

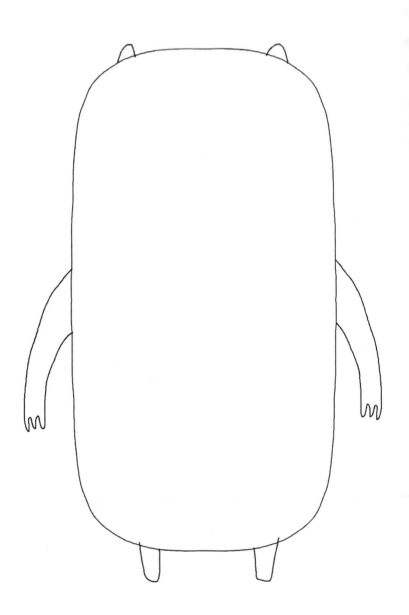

GO FOR A WALK! LEAVE YOUR PHONE AT HOME!

AUTOWRITING

Myles Have you ever tried automatic writing?

Greg Is that that thing where you write stuff without thinking and don't stop?

Myles That's right.

Greg I've not. Why don't you tell me about it on this page?

Myles I will.

Grab a book. Open at a random page. Point at a word.

Write down the word. Now write down the two words before. Now the two words afterward.

Now use this as your title. Begin writing and don't stop for five minutes. Don't think about what you are writing too much. Be very instinctive. Just write. Write whatever stuff comes into your head. It doesn't have to make sense. Just write.

If you're struggling to get ideas flowing, this can be a fun exercise to unblock your creative constipation.

Most of the time you end up writing a load of old rubbish, but occasionally something really interesting pops out. Here's some automatic writing from my archive!

My five words were "**Under Got You My Skin.**"

Here's what came out of my subconscious. It's a bit weird, but interesting!

Under Got You My Skin

Under the sea is a giant mass of blue, waving silicon
that rustles and weaves through the water like a
mesh of gelatin. It's a kind of skin that lives inside
the sea and touches and changes everything that it
meets. That is how the legend of mermaids began.
A creature was created when a man called Nigel De
Haviland jumped from a shipwreck onto a burning
barge and then into the sea below. He fell into the
seaskin and was wrapped in it tightly. It squeezed
all his breath from him, but he wasn't troubled since
in that instant he found he had gills at his throat, a
tail where his legs once were, and that the burns on
his skin had healed.

The cold, icy water no longer rasped against his flesh, as it developed a thin but warm layer of blubber . . . and he was away: a new man. And more than a new man. He was a new species. And so many more sea people were created. The seaskin is now old and very few new merpeople are made, and many of the old ones are either dead or live so deep in the dark oceans that no one ever sees them. Some returned to the land and lost their fishy ways, and lived out their long extended lives among us. For the seaskin also transferred long life to the merpeople.

There is some suggestion that the seaskin will be renewed, that a new skin is forming even now at the bottom of some seabed, waiting for the time it will detach and grow and slip among the currents, working its natural magic on the plants and creatures that encounter it. There is also another seaskin, but that is to be feared. It absorbs, rather than gives or changes. There are people given gills and sustenance who have attached to that skin, but they are permanently fixed to it as it flutters and shivers through the depths. It is like a giant, dirty piece of Scotch tape that picks up all the waste and filth that it comes across. It too is old and has many horrid layers of encrustation.

When it rises to the surface a great effusion of stinking, eviscerated, sulfurous, noxious, rotting stench is released and gases any birds, fishermen or other air creatures and can even kill if a deep enough breath is taken. Legend speaks of a day when the two seaskins will meet, and who knows what will happen then. Perhaps one will absorb the other. Perhaps a new skin will be formed with new and wonderful or terrible or both properties. Only time will tell and our time is so brief I do not expect to be the one to discover the truth of that moment.

AUTOWRITING

Now you have a go—try to fill both pages:

Television

What is the stupidest name you can think
of for a reality TV show?

_____

What is the stupidest name you can think
of for a new soap opera?

_____

What is the stupidest name you can think
of for a new comedy show?

_____

SIT QUIETLY AND STARE OUT THE WINDOW FOR HALF AN HOUR.

A BRIEF HISTORY OF IDEAS

* Part Two *

If opportunity
doesn't knock,
build a door.
—Milton Berle

What's beyond the door?

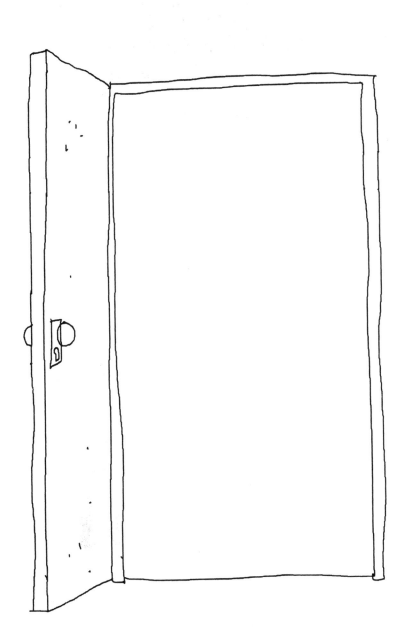

Retelling old stories

Sometimes it's good to use an old and existing story to kick off some new ideas. Try telling the story in a different way.

**Once upon a time
there were three little pigs . . .**

HOW TO HAVE IDEAS

Tidy up
Sweep up
Clean up
Afterward you may feel
at one with the universe.

Draw to the music

Find a piece of **rock music** and draw your picture below—let your hand move to the music and see what happens:

No, we are not advocating alcohol as a creative lubricant. Often it has precisely the opposite effect. This wineglass is a metaphor. Sometimes when you've been working hard, or overdoing it, or even making up too many ideas, you feel empty, like you've poured away all your creativity. You need to fill yourself back up, but how? Inspire yourself again. Read a book. Go somewhere interesting for the weekend. Go to a museum. A gallery. Watch a classic film. Talk to an inspiring friend.

You'll find that in time your wineglass is full of creative juice once again.

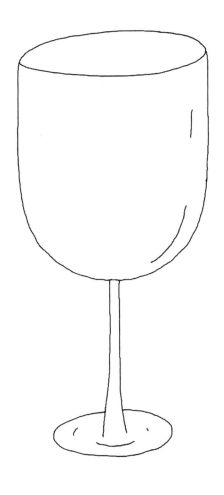

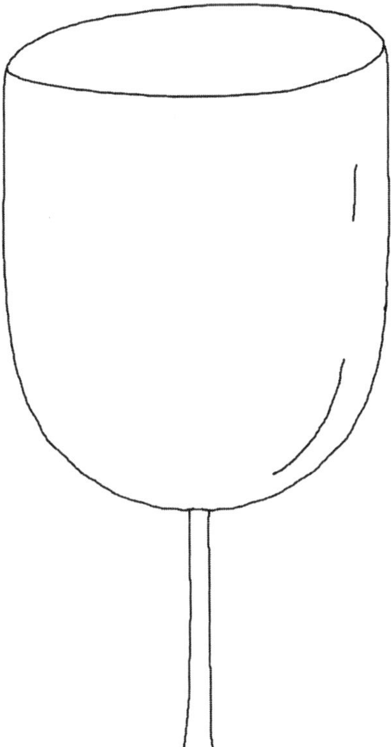

What's in the glass?

HOW NOT TO HAVE IDEAS

Wait for an e-mail to come in so you can answer it straightaway.

Complete the picture:

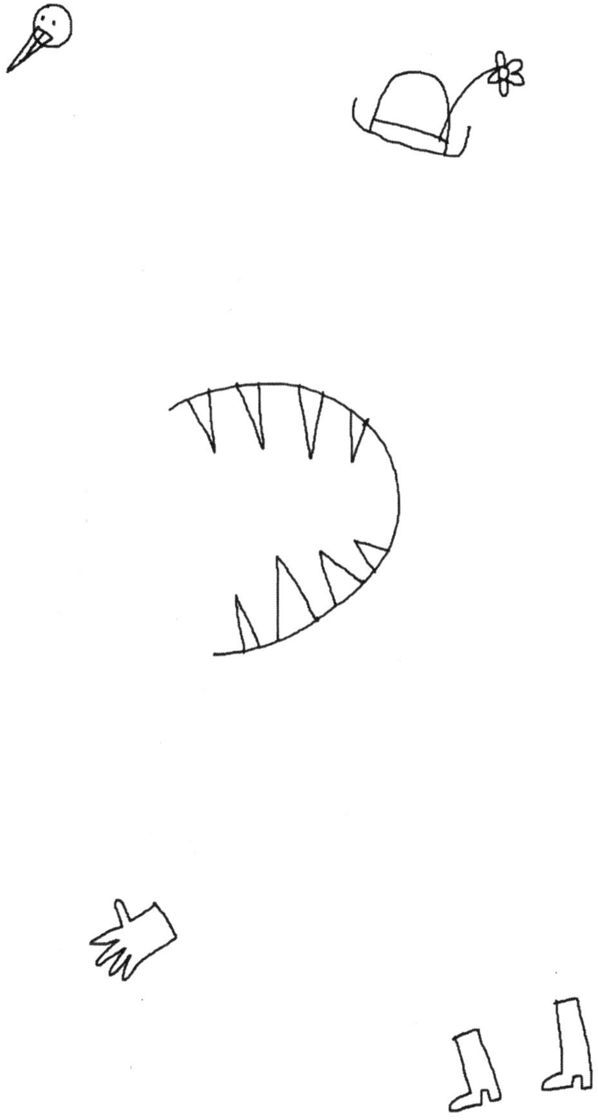

Complete the story

No! Stop! Put that back in the . . .

_____

_____

_____

_____

_____

_____

_____

_____

_____

_____

_____

_____

_____

Give this character a name.

Now fill in the bubbles. What are the good things about them? What are their flaws? What's their family history? What do they worry about? What is their ambition?

Complete the picture:

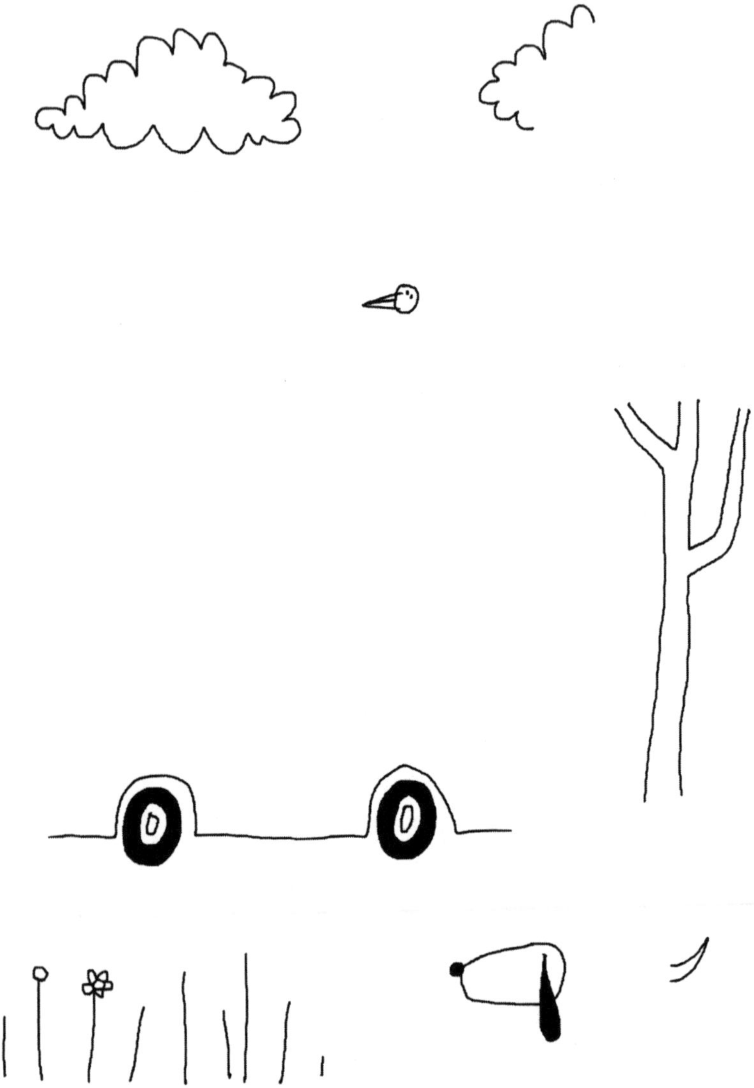

HOW TO HAVE IDEAS

**Relax. If at all possible just relax.
Ideas will occur naturally.**

Congratulations, you are now ruler of the world.

What are the first ten laws you are going to pass?

1. _____

2. _____

3. _____

4. _____

5. _____

6. _____

7. _____

8. _____

9. _____

10. _____

CARDBOARD BOX

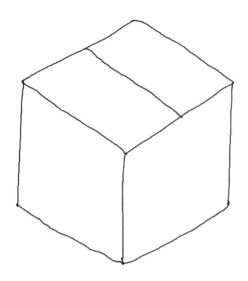

Here is a cardboard box.

What's in the box?

Come up with an advertising
slogan for it.

Now decorate it.

NEW WAYS TO WAKE UP

The Feather Clock
The Porcupine Piston
The Symphonic Expenditure
The Elephant Shower

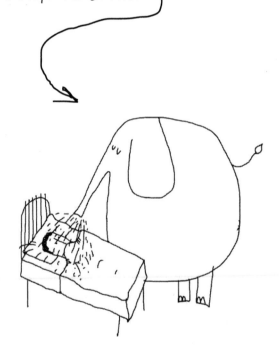

Write (or draw) your ideas here:

A BRIEF
HISTORY
OF IDEAS
* Part Three *

My ideas usually
come not from my
desk writing but in
the midst of living.
—**Anaïs Nin**

COLOR ME IN

Now give me a name: _____

OPPOSITES

Sometimes when coming up with characters it's useful
to make them opposites. This can create interesting
juxtapositions and stimulate possibilities for conversations
and action between them. Below we've used two simple
shapes as a starting point. We've ended up with a tattooed
American truck driver and an old lady from Bexhill-on-Sea.

OPPOSITES

Create two opposing characters from the shapes below:

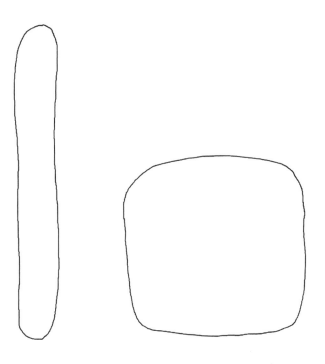

HOW NOT TO HAVE IDEAS
IN YOUR MINDBOX

Cardboard Tube

Waste time talking into a
cardboard tube listening
to yourself with a weird
echoey voice. Myles did
this on several occasions
while (not) writing this
book.

Character blanks

This time, try using circles
to create multiple characters:

Maps

We both loved maps in books as kids and we still like creating them. Start with the house below and draw your own landscape over the two pages. Will it be a town or a village? Will there be mountains, forests, or rivers? It's your choice. Once it's done, all kinds of story ideas may occur to you.

N
W
E
S

A BRIEF HISTORY OF IDEAS

* Part Four *

Anything becomes
interesting if you
look at it long
enough.

—Gustave Flaubert

Take Gustave Flaubert's advice—find something ordinary and stare at it. Let it generate some ideas either to draw or write about below.

HOW TO HAVE IDEAS IN YOUR MINDBOX

Go for a walk. Walk your dog. Walk someone else's
dog. Walk an imaginary dog. Just go for a walk.
Sometimes sitting at a desk is the worst for ideas.

HEADLINES

Cut out some words from newspaper headlines
and try to make up a new headline.

CHEESE Man *EATS* Head

Stick yours in below:

PLAYLIST

*Create a playlist for a
desert-based road movie:*

1. _____

2. _____

3. _____

4. _____

5. _____

6. _____

7. _____

8. _____

9. _____

10. _____

Who are the travelers in the movie?

Where do they start the journey?

Where are they going?

What do they find when they get there?

Drawing with your eyes closed

Draw a character with your eyes closed. It will probably look really wonky, but with a bit of creativity you can then transform it into a more clearly rendered drawing.

Before   **After**

Try it below:

SPLAT!

Use the ink trails to create some characters
and locations:

From this . . .

. . . to this.

Try it below:

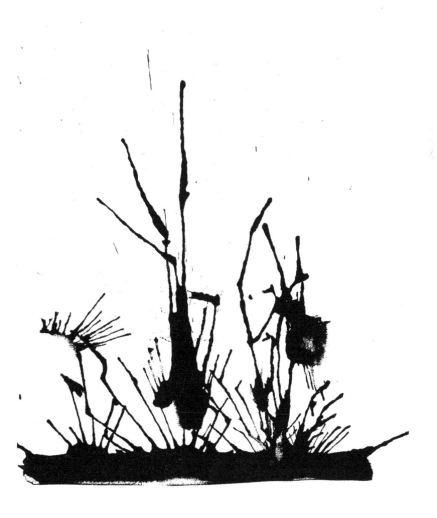

Squiggle pic—find some more characters:

Friend or foe?

Draw your own hero and their nemesis:

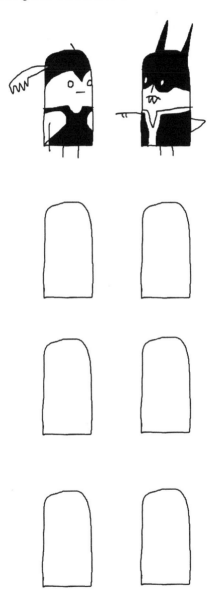

Fill in the speech bubbles:

Repeat shapes

Sometimes it can be good to sit and repeatedly draw the same shape until the page is full. This is strangely calming. Try it yourself below:

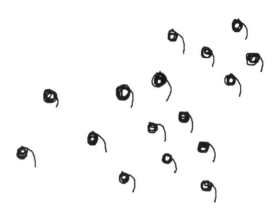

Sci-fi city

By using simple curved shapes and then adding some detail you can create your own sci-fi city.

Try it below:

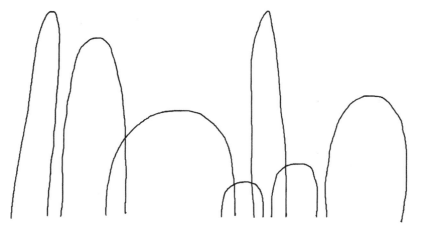

Now draw your own curves and make a new city:

OPPOSITES

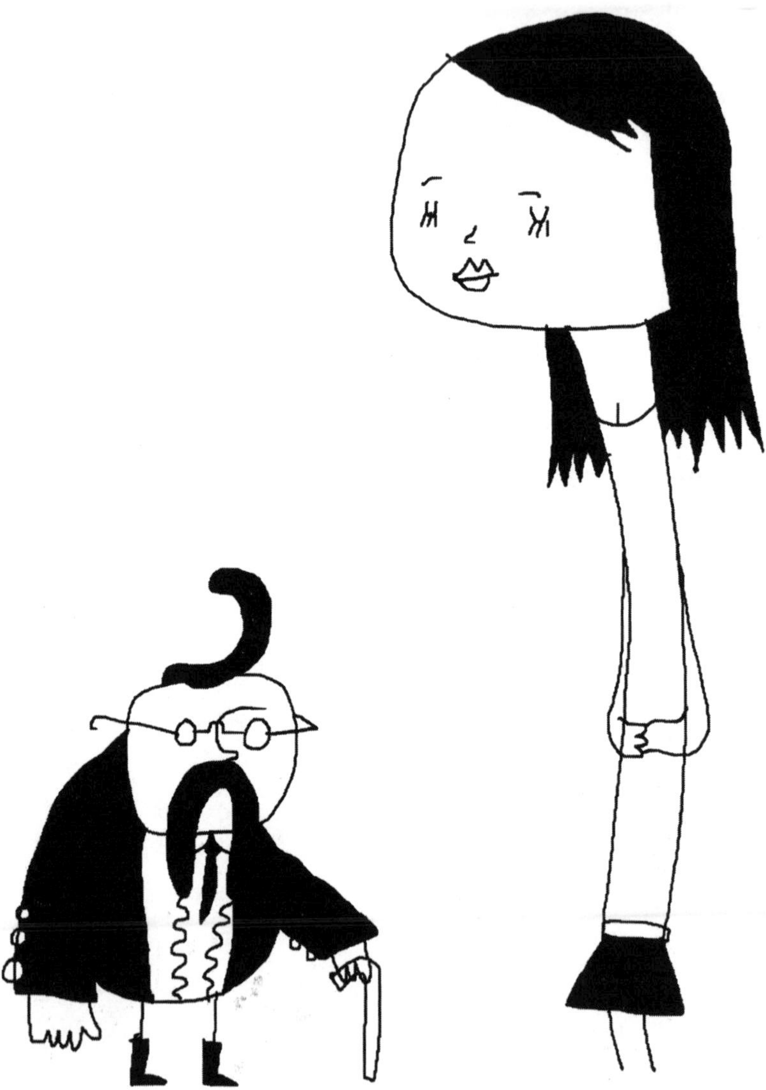

Create two opposing characters from the shapes below:

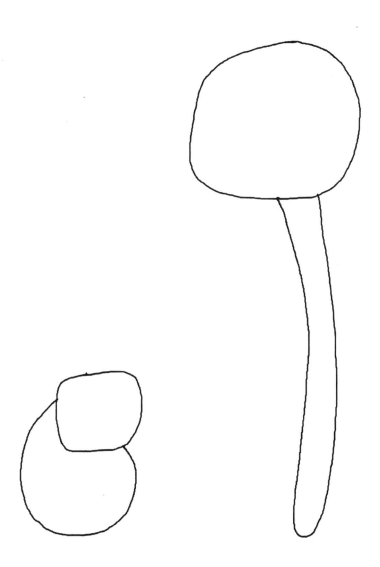

Coffee-shop sketching

Capture the essence of people sitting near you, or passing by. Try to draw the people who come and go quickly. See how well you can capture them in a short amount of time.

Try it below:

PLAYLIST

Create a playlist for a horror movie:

1. _____

2. _____

3. _____

4. _____

5. _____

6. _____

7. _____

8. _____

9. _____

10. _____

WHAT SCARES YOU THE MOST?

_ _ _ _ _ _ _ _ _ _ _ _ _ _ _ _

_ _ _ _ _ _ _ _ _ _ _ _ _ _ _ _

WHERE DOES YOUR FEAR COME FROM?

_ _ _ _ _ _ _ _ _ _ _ _ _ _ _ _

_ _ _ _ _ _ _ _ _ _ _ _ _ _ _ _

WHAT COULD DEFEAT YOUR FEAR?

_ _ _ _ _ _ _ _ _ _ _ _ _ _ _ _

_ _ _ _ _ _ _ _ _ _ _ _ _ _ _ _

Complete the story

Where's my shoe? I put it on the bench. Now that it's gone,
I'm going to have to . . .

_____

_____

_____

_____

_____

_____

_____

_____

_____

_____

_____

_____

_____

_____

Complete the picture:

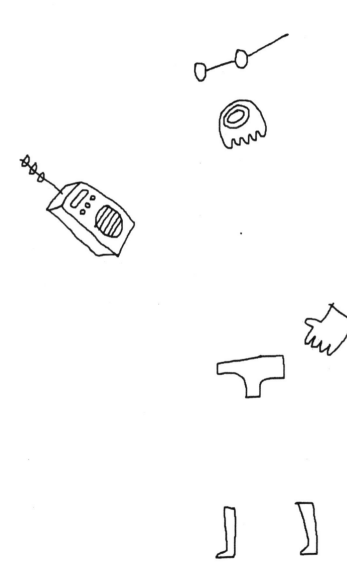

A new alphabet

Create new symbols for the alphabet.

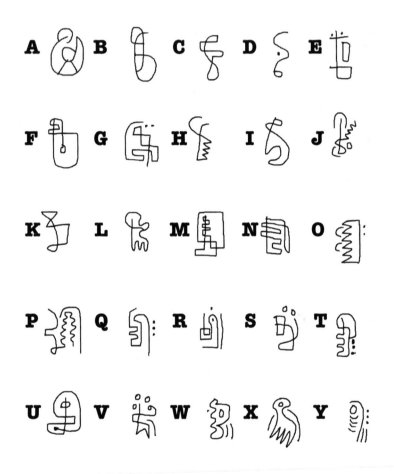

Now you try it:

A   B   C   D   E

F   G   H   I   J

K   L   M   N   O

P   Q   R   S   T

U   V   W   X   Y

Z

Left-hand drawing

Here's my effort . . .

Left-hand drawing

Your turn:

Faces on domestic household items

It's amazing what you can do with a set of eyebrows.
Draw some features on the items below:

Draw some items from your house and give them some features—bring them to life!

Geometric coloring in

A great way of clearing the mind.

Geometric drawing

Try it below:

Design your own set of
Russian dolls

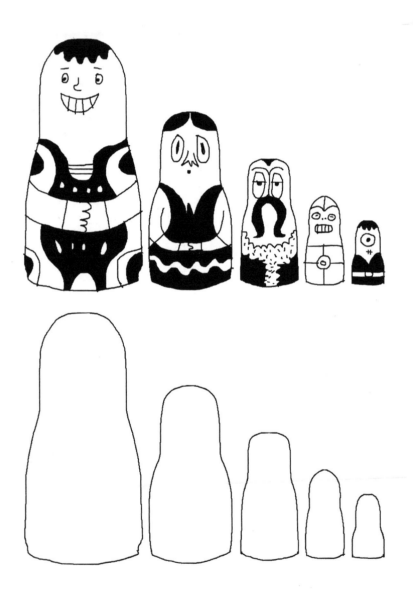

Draw to the music

Find a piece of **dance music** and draw your picture below—this time, let your hand do the dancing, and see what it creates:

Unusual architecture

Wherever you live there will be one building that is a little odd—one that doesn't quite sit with the others. Draw this building and imagine it in a new setting. On a mountain or on an island in a lake. Who lives there? What's their story?

Draw your picture below:

Design and color an alien being

Here's ours, you can color it in:

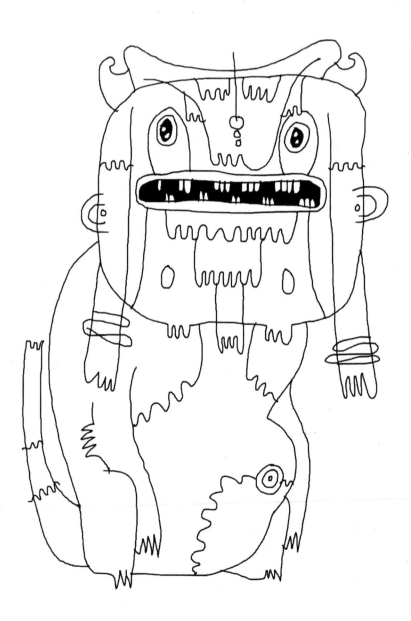

Design yours below:

PLAYLIST

*Create a playlist for a
movie about your childhood:*

1. _____

2. _____

3. _____

4. _____

5. _____

6. _____

7. _____

8. _____

9. _____

10. _____

What's your earliest childhood memory?

CHARACTER BLANKS

Here's another shape you can use to create multiple characters:

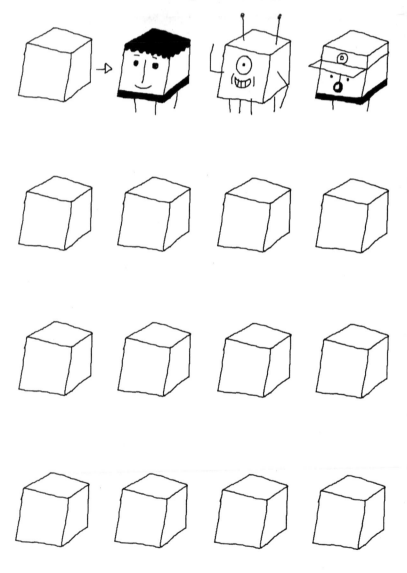

Who's talking? What are they saying?

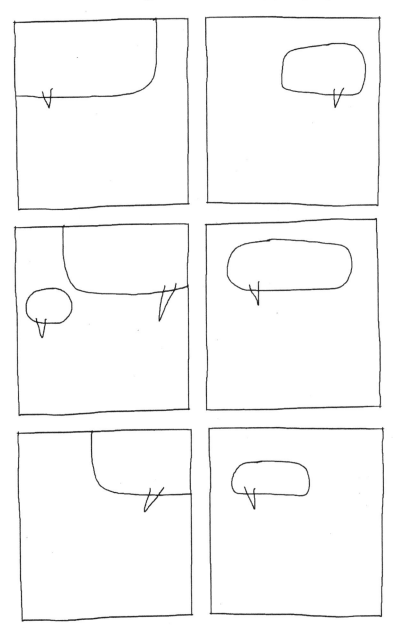

Draw this criminal mastermind:

Jemima Grindface

Draw this criminal mastermind:

Skeleton Ben

HOW NOT TO HAVE IDEAS

Go on a long shopping excursion for a minor
household item.

HOW TO HAVE IDEAS

What would your trip to the shops have been like in:

A ZOMBIE APOCALYPSE?

A Cloak of Invisibility?

The Worst Snowstorm of the Century?

Your Pajamas?

Halloween Night?

A Tank?

A Total Eclipse of the Sun?

Fill in the panels:

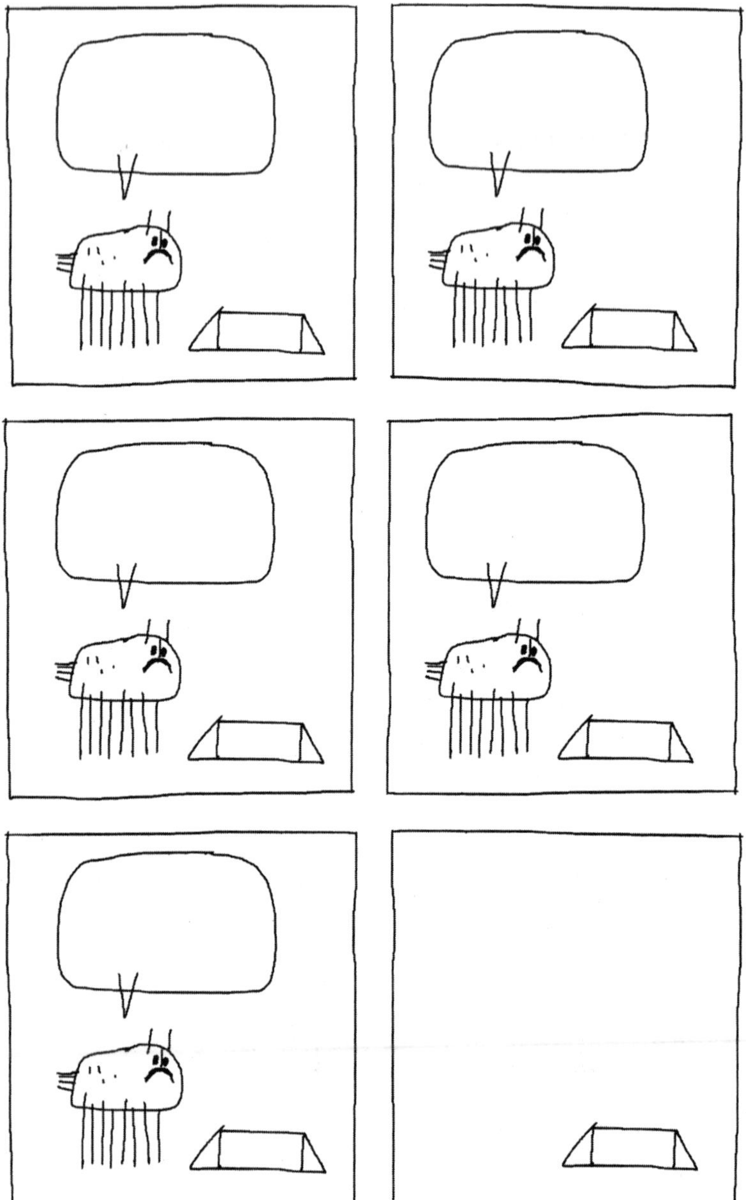

WATCH A MOVIE OR VIDEO FROM A RANDOMLY SELECTED COUNTRY.

SPLAT!

Use the ink splats below to create some
characters or objects:

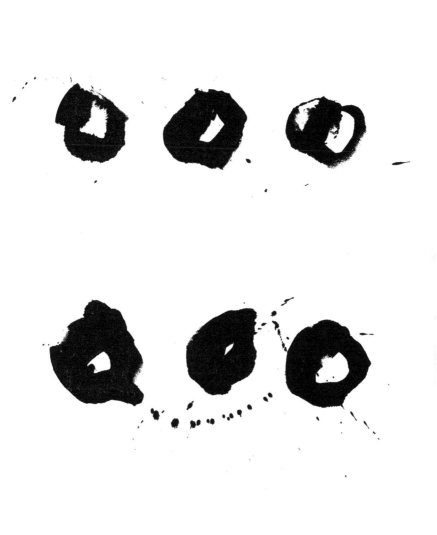

DRAW A POP STAR

What's their name? _____

What's their bestselling hit? _____

STOP!

Close your eyes and count to

100

Visualize the numbers as you do so.

Copycat

Try drawing the mirror image to complete this picture:

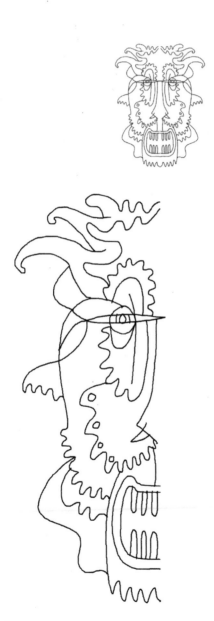

Design your own T-shirt:

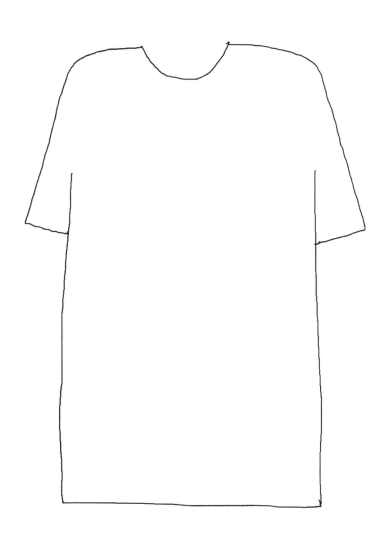

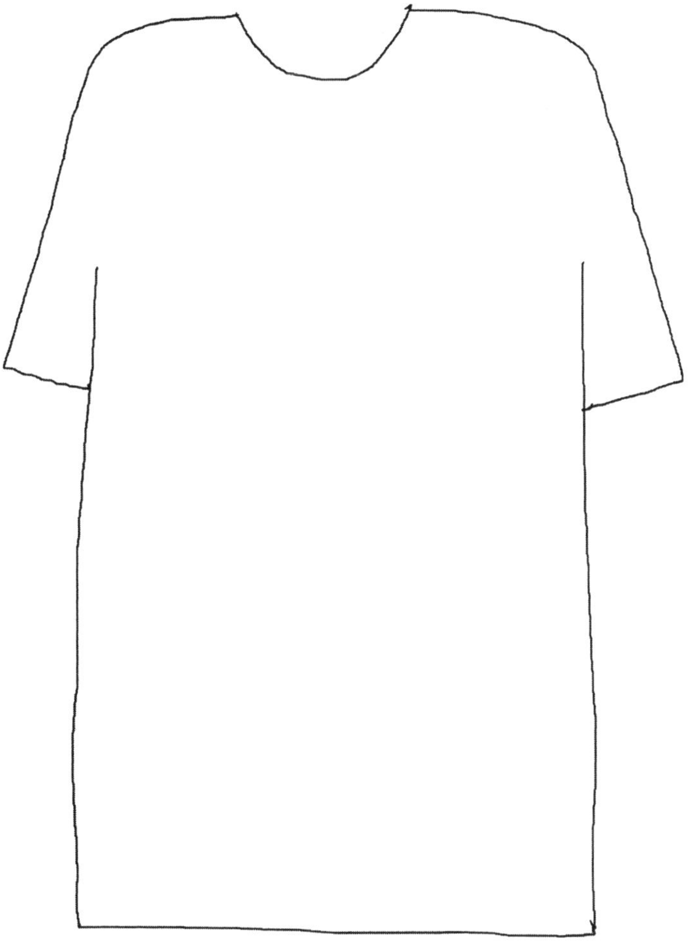

Finally, remember this. Sometimes it's good to create something because you have a burning desire to say something profound.

Sometimes it's good to create something . . .

JUST FOR THE HELL OF IT!